off to the Movies

written by Kelly Gaffney

illustrated by Wesley Lowe

Monday, 11th June

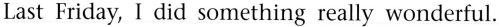

Dear Diary,

Last Friday, I did something really wonderful.
I went to a *movie set*
with my big brother, Tom.
Tom is an *actor* and he has been
in three movies.
I thought acting was an easy job,
so Tom wanted to show me
all the things that an actor has to do.

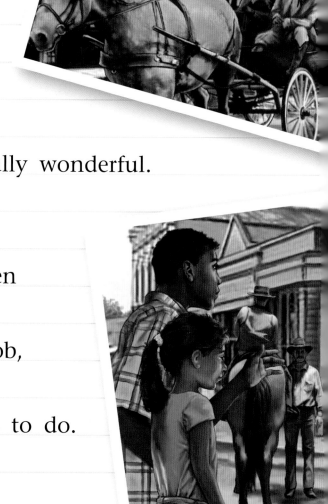

When we arrived at the movie set,
there were people everywhere.
The movie was about a large family
who lived a long time ago.
It was at a time when there were
no cars or *computers*.
Some people were dressed
for their part in the movie.
I saw people riding around on *horses*,
and I even saw a horse and cart.

As I followed Tom around,
I couldn't believe it.
The movie set looked just like a *town*
from a long time ago.
The roads were made of dirt
and there were lots of *wooden buildings*.
They looked very old, but Tom said
they had only been made
three months ago.

Tom took me to a large shed.

Inside the shed were lots of rooms.

They looked just like the rooms
you would find in an old house.

Tom told me that this is where
the *indoor* parts of the movie are made.

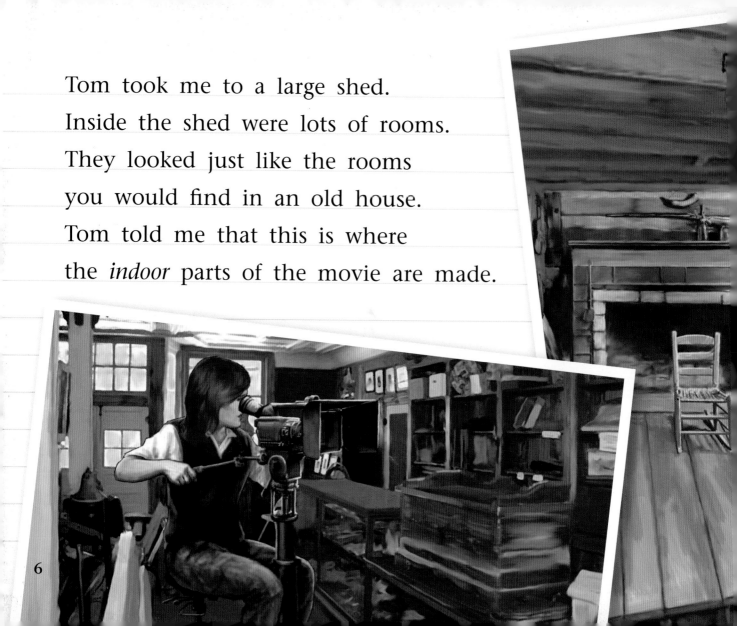

Next, Tom took me to where
all the *costume*s are kept.
They were very different
from the *clothes* we wear.
There were lots of long dresses
and hats for the ladies and girls.
I saw funny *trousers, jackets*
and hats for the men and boys.
I tried on a beautiful red dress.
It was just my size!

Then Tom took me to the place
where the actors get their hair
and *make-up* done.
I saw a boy sitting near
a *mirror* with bright lights.
A lady was putting make-up on him.
Even the men and boys
have to wear make-up in a movie!

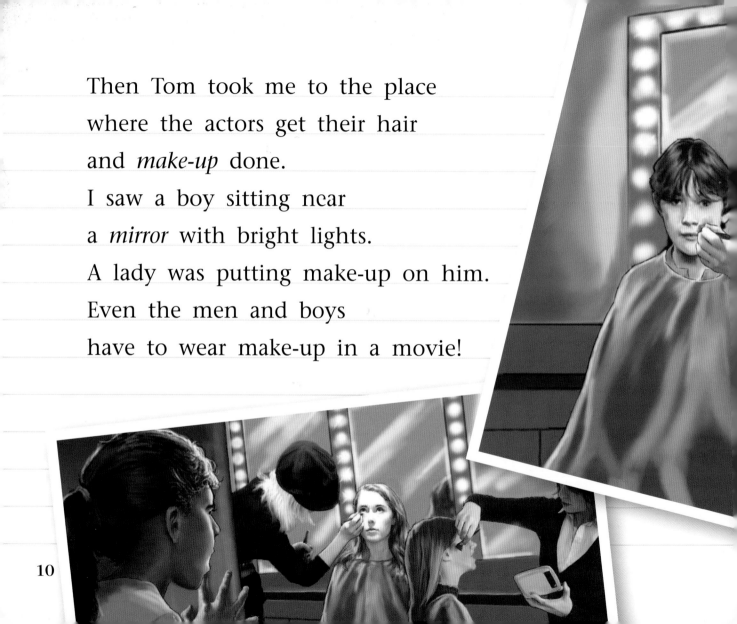

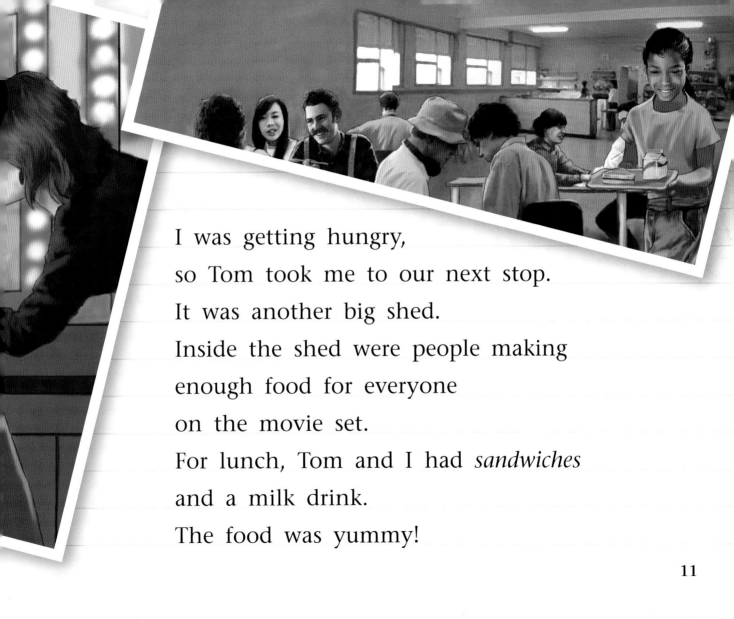

I was getting hungry,
so Tom took me to our next stop.
It was another big shed.
Inside the shed were people making
enough food for everyone
on the movie set.
For lunch, Tom and I had *sandwiches*
and a milk drink.
The food was yummy!

After lunch, we went to the place
where the movie was being filmed.
Tom told me to be very quiet.
There were *cameras*, *microphones*
and bright lights above the actors.
Sometimes the actors
had to go over their lines
many times — until everyone
got their lines just right.

Tom showed me some people
who are called *movie extras*.
These people are also dressed up
but their job is to walk around and talk
in the background of the movie.
Tom told me that some of these people
want to be actors, and that being
a movie extra was a good place to start.

Tom and I had a really great day.
I think I might ask Mum and Dad
if I can be a movie extra.
I really want to be an actor like Tom.
Being an actor may be hard work,
but it's lots of fun, too!

Picture Glossary

actor

costumes

make-up

movie set

town

cameras

horses

microphones

sandwiches

trousers

clothes

indoor

mirror

wooden buildings

computers

jackets

movie extras